Buckets to Pipelines

The 7 Principles of Prosperity That Will Show Dentists How They Can Finally Get Out of the Chair

By Matt Kennedy and Nate Schott, DDS

Copyright © 2014 Matt Kennedy and Dr. Nate Schott, DDS
All rights reserved.
ISBN-10: 1502839849
ISBN-13: 978-1502839848

Here's What's Inside...

5   Forward: Why Dentists Can't Get out of the Chair... by Dr. Schott

10 Buckets to Pipelines!

22 The 7 Principles of Prosperity Every Dentist Should Know...*

22 Prosperity Principle #1: THINK...Think Like an Entrepreneur...

23 Prosperity Principle #2: SEE...Avoid Financial Tunnel Vision...

23 Prosperity Principle #3: MEASURE...Always Measure Opportunity Costs...

24 Prosperity Principle #4: FLOW...Don't Focus on Net Worth alone...

25 Prosperity Principle #5: CONTROL...Control of Your Capital Is More Important than Rate of Return...

28 Prosperity Principle #6: MOVE...Act Like a Bank...move money through assets not to assets

29 Prosperity Principle #7: MULTIPLY...Efficiency Allows Money to Multiply Many Times Over...

36 Here's How to Get Out of the Chair and Into Your Life...

37 About the Authors

* For more information about The 7 Principles of Prosperity or the Prosperity Economics Movement mentioned later in this book, please visit www.prosperitypeaks.com.

Forward

Why Dentists Can't Get Out of the Chair...

Matt Kennedy and I love to help dentists change the way they think about their practice. We want them out of the chair and into their life. The issue at hand is, as a dentist, we are trained to do one thing and do one thing very well. We are able to do dentistry. We take care of our patients. We are taught at dental school to do all of the things we need to do to restore people's mouths back to a healthy dentition as we call it, but also so it's functionally and cosmetically sound. But the truth is, as we go through life and go through the cycles of practice what we find is it is really hard work. It is not only hard work but it's very taxing on the body; it is taxing on the mind. It wears you down.

When we get out of dental school, we are expected the minute we go into practice to be able to run a practice as well as we can do dentistry. One thing we are not taught is how to run a successful practice. There is more to running a dental practice than working with the patients. What about the dynamics of a practice? We have to know how to make sure we have the appropriate staff, the appropriate procedures and at the end of the day, it needs to be profitable. We are not taught any of this mission critical stuff in school. Some of us are able to learn these skills and some of us don't ever learn them. A lot of dentists get to a point where they get so burned out, they've tried everything, they don't know essentially what's happening or where all this is going?

Our mission is to help dentists do what they do best. Let's discover what you do well and use your unique ability, as Dan Sullivan refers to it. Discover what your unique ability is and stay in that at least 70-80% of the time and don't do anything else. When you do this, your practice becomes more profitable and you are able to enjoy much more time away from the practice. I haven't practiced dentistry now for two years in the chair because I've discovered my unique ability. I've been in practice for 23 years.

Matt is going to teach the principles of how to bank your own growth instead of worrying about going out to get loans with stingy financial institutions. Becoming my own bank has helped me in a big way.

Why do dentists have so much trouble getting out of the chair? Dentists are taught that if we do things well, patients are going to come to us and they will continue to patronize us. However the truth is we live in a society today that is a time driven society. People do things based on the time they have. We have been conditioned now with the internet and hand-held devices that we can have whatever we need within 24 hours. In this kind of society, the traditional way a dentist delivers his or her services is out of date. We have to change the delivery mode. We are no longer competing with the dentist down the street. We are competing with Wal-Mart and Amazon. We are no longer competing on quality or price, we are competing on accessibility. So the delivery system change I have found most effective is focusing on when we do dentistry not on how we do dentistry. My practices are open 7 am to 9 pm 7 days a week. Our schedule is most full from 7 am to 9 am and then from about 5 pm until 9 pm. The evidence is clear.

People, especially people with good jobs that can pay for their dental work, want before work and after work or before school or after school appointments.

Time is very important to these people, so no longer do they just want to do one filling at a time or one restoration at a time. They are able to do more because they can afford to do it and time is precious to them. They don't want to be away from their families or their friends or just their recreational activities. We found that expanding our hours really works. We started a year ago with one practice and now we have three practices up and going because of the tremendous amount of growth and the need that has been required to meet the demand of the patients.

Again, we are told if we do dentistry well, people will come to us and stay with us. If that were the case, every dentist would have a building the size of a hospital because none of their patients would ever leave them. At the end of 30 or 40 years, those patients would still be coming in for their hygiene appointments. They'd still be coming in to see their dentist for regular checkups. This is not the case. They are going other places and it is not because we do bad dentistry. It is because it's more convenient, or it's more affordable, or they are able to get the care that they need and really the care that they want.

My guiding mission has changed. It is "what's best for the patient is best for the practice". Give the patient what they want, they will trust you with what they need and they will allow you to do those things that they need. Many times we want to use the latest, greatest, technique or the latest greatest gadget to show the patient we are different than the dentist down the road. The truth of the matter is the patient just wants to be taken care of. They want to be treated like a human being. They want to be seen when they want to be seen. They are not interested in being seen when we want to see them. The model of being open from 8:30 to 5, four days a week is going by the wayside because the patient has options now.

We understand this and implement it in many other areas of society. We just haven't fully implemented it into all of healthcare. The traditional healthcare model is starting to change too. You are seeing walk-in clinics; hospitals are opening in new ways and physicians are changing the way that they run their practices. Dentists are going to have to change and expand their model. In order to expand the model, we will need to have the money and the funding to be able to grow. That's what Matt's financial principles bring to the table. His financial principles combined with my practice principles, work tremendously well together.

You should be offering services when the patient wants and needs to be in the chair. If you are going to work 8 hours in a day, what does it matter which 8 hours you are going to work? I'm saying come in at 4 or 5 o'clock and work until 9 o'clock and do that four days a week. Change around your staff or add other doctors in your office in those before work and after work hours that you can't get to. Allow your practice to really become a business and a place where patients want to go.

Let me take a moment to set up the rest of the book and talk about what I believe about finances. Traditional financial planning has failed the dentist miserably. Those of us that have been in practice for 20 or 30 years were told that our retirement would be achieved by saving in 401(k)s and in selling the practice. The problem is we can't sell the practice for what it is really worth. The young dentist can't buy the practice because they can't afford to. Many of them have anywhere from three to five hundred thousand dollars of debt just from dental school alone. Banks won't loan to these young men and women just getting out of school, so there is no buyer waiting in the wings. Let's make the asset or the practice work for the dentist now, not just later when he wants to sell and retire.

As older dentists, we've got to become mentors and visionaries. We've got to become sages that pass down the wisdom to younger dentists. I am passionate and firmly believe that we that by not selling our practices but by turning our practices into self-managing businesses. This lets us be in a position where we don't have to do the work in the business but we can work on the business. Matt is going to talk about how the dentist can unlock assets he has now in order to make this happen sooner rather than later.

- Dr. Nate Schott

Buckets to Pipelines!

Nate: Good afternoon, this is Dr. Nate Schott and I'm excited to be here with Matt Kennedy. Matt is going to be sharing with us today his thoughts and ideas on how dentists can finally get out of the chair. Welcome, Matt.

Matt: Thank you, Nate. Glad to be here.

Nate: Why did you want to write a book on how dentists can get out of the chair?

Matt: I believe dentists have been trapped by traditional financial planning in a model that will not and is not working for them. Robert Kiyosaki, in his books, tells a great story about a town that lost its water supply. The town council got together and they awarded the job of resupplying water to the town to two different businessmen.

The first businessman ran out and bought as many buckets as he could. His strategy was very simple, very effective and very lucrative. He simply took the buckets to the reservoir, filled up the buckets and then emptied the buckets in the reservoirs of every house. This was very lucrative for him. He had a corner on the market. He started making money immediately.

The second businessman decided to take a different approach to the problem. He commissioned a feasibility study. He hired engineers, architects and they studied what the cost would be and the effectiveness of building a pipeline from a reservoir to the town. After about six months, he finally got the results from the feasibility study and he realized he was going to have to invest some capital to make his dream happen and he went out and got investors. He borrowed money and they started the project. It took them another six months to build the pipeline.

A year after the council awarded him the project, his pipeline was up and running. For a small connection fee and a small monthly service fee, every person in the town could now connect to the pipeline and have continuous running water. We can see what happened. The first businessman was out of business very quickly. As a result of his strategic planning the second businessman enjoyed a steady stream of income throughout the rest of his life.

The traditional financial planning model for the dentist is the same bucket model as our first business above. Fill a bucket, in this case, maybe it's a 401k or a profit sharing plan or some type of investment, fill the bucket up, let it accumulate, let it accumulate, let it accumulate and then at some point we're going to empty the bucket.

The idea is if we have enough buckets in place we can replace our current income. The reality however is the plan that traditional planners have given the dentists isn't working because it was based on a pretty big assumption. The assumption is if we did put money into a 401(k) or a profit sharing plan, take it out of the business, lock it up over here in this qualified plan that it will grow.

They plug this assumption into some software which assumes some type of growth based on past performance and base all future hopes and dreams on this past performance. They go on to add that the 401(k) bucket combined with the bucket from selling your dental practice will be plenty to replace your current lifestyle. Well the truth is that model is not working. 401(k)s have a tendency to get devastated. They're not growing in the way that was assumed. Most dentists that I see are fifty, fifty-five years old with only a million to a million and a half dollars sitting in a qualified plan. On top of that, dental practices aren't selling.

My experience has been that new dentists coming out of dental school have way too much debt to want to get into borrowing more money to go out and buy a practice. The value just isn't there. We are seeing that there's not the patient loyalty there used to be with dentists, or with the dental practice so if a new dentist comes in and buys the practice, it's not necessarily a given that all of those patients are going to stay. What's happening is dental practices are selling for sixty to seventy cents on the dollar of last year's gross revenue. If you have a dental practice which is grossing two million dollars, well sixty to seventy cents on the dollar is not that much money, certainly not enough for the dentists to retire like they were promised.

If you combine the 401(k) with what they can get for selling their dental practice, after taxes, there's no way that they can replace a current lifestyle of three, four or five hundred thousand dollars a year which is what many dentists are enjoying right now. The old model is simply not working. It's not working, not because the traditional financial planners are bad but because the financial institutions that they work for are the ones crafting the message that they're giving to the dentists.

The financial institutions are telling the dentists to build net worth. That's what the bucket strategy really is. It's a strategy accumulating assets somewhere that you can put on a balance sheet to show some kind of net worth. But at some point you're going to convert that net worth to cash flow to replace your income. Why are the financial institutions telling us to do that? They're telling us to do that because typically when we build net worth that net worth gets stored where? It gets stored with the financial institutions, banks, insurance companies, mutual fund companies, et cetera.

The financial institution then does what with all that money? They use it to create cash flow. That's all a financial institution does. They rent your money at a certain interest rate. They pay you two percent or three percent and then they go out and sell money at a higher interest rate. This creates cash flow for the bank. They loan out your money in a mortgage. They get payments back as cash flow. They loan your money out in a car loan, they get cash flow back. So financial institutions are doing the exact opposite of what they're telling us to do because they don't want us to know that cash flow is more important than net worth. Quite frankly, the financial institutions invented the bucket strategy in order to get people to do what's best for the financial institution, not what's best for the people.

Nate: Very interesting Matt. So if the dentist had a million dollars in their 401(k), what kind of cash flow would that equate to them on an ongoing basis?

Matt: Well here's the problem. Is a million dollars in a 401(k) or any before-tax qualified plan really a million dollars?

Let's say we sit down with your CPA and you have a million dollars in a 401(k) balance. I will look at the CPA and say, "You listed this 401k as an asset. What's the liability on that 401(k)?" The CPA will look at me and say, "I don't understand what you are saying." I say, "That money has never been taxed so there is a tax liability." Having a million dollars in the 401(k) means nothing because the dentist doesn't have a million dollars.

What matters is the tax bracket the dentist is in when he or she takes the money out? What are taxes like in the United States? Do you believe taxes in the future are going to be lower, the same, or higher? If I have a million dollars sitting there and I'm in a forty percent tax bracket, I really don't have a million dollars. If I pulled it all out at one time, I'd have six hundred thousand dollars, right? If I took a million dollars and tried to convert it into cash flow, the missing piece there is what type of tax situation am I in? This is a real key point because what happens is dentists make financial decisions in their own compartment. Let me explain, they make decisions like this. A dentist has to make a house decision, right? He has to decide where he is going to live and how he is going to finance that house? Is he going to use a fifteen year mortgage or a thirty year mortgage, or a ten year mortgage? He uses whatever criteria he uses to make that decision and once they make that decision they never think about it again.

In addition to the mortgage decision, they have a retirement saving decision. Should they do a 401(k) profit sharing plan? If so, how much should they put in there? He uses whatever criteria he uses to make that decision and then he moves on and doesn't think about it again. Then they've got these car decisions. How is he going to purchase cars? Is he going to finance? Is he going to pay cash? Is he going to lease them through the business? Again he uses whatever criteria he uses to make this decision and moves on. College planning is the same thing. It goes on and on and on. What happens is all of those financial decisions are made in their own compartment as if each of those decisions has no effect on any of the other decisions. This just simply isn't true.

Let me explain why this is. Let's say that the dentist takes a fifteen year mortgage on his house. The way a fifteen year mortgage works is it's usually five hundred or a thousand dollars more per month on a monthly basis than a thirty year mortgage. What's happening with that extra thousand dollars that you're sending back to the bank? The bank is turning it around and using it to create more cash flow, so the bank loves the fifteen year mortgage. But what's happening internally in the fifteen year mortgage? Every time you make that extra thousand dollar payment the principal owed is going down. What's also going down? Every time my principal balance goes down the amount of interest that the bank is charging me goes down. People look at that and think that's a really good thing.

Under many conditions mortgage interest is tax deductible. Every time I make the 15 year mortgage payment my principal is going down and the interest I am charged goes down. When the amount of interest I am charged goes down, so does the tax deduction. Principle is going down, interest is going down and taxes are going up. I'm getting up in the morning. I am going to see patients so I can put money in one pocket which is the mortgage and I'm losing a tax deduction to do it.

At the same time, I'm seeing more patients and putting money into the 401(k)/profit sharing plan because my accountant told me I'd get a tax deduction there. Do you see what I'm doing? Really this is like driving down the highway of your financial life with one foot on the brake and one foot on the gas. In one area I'm losing a tax deduction as fast as possible and in another area I'm trying to gain a tax deduction as fast as possible. That's an uncoordinated decision.

So what we are doing here is shining a light on this for the dentists. Is there a way for them to pay their house off in fifteen years or less and keep the tax deduction as high as possible throughout the entire fifteen years? When I am making uncoordinated financial decisions it really becomes devastating to my financial landscape. Why is it devastating? It's devastating because every time I lose a dollar, I'm not only losing that dollar but I am losing the ability to earn interest on that dollar. This is called lost opportunity cost.

When I'm losing that tax deduction in the mortgage, I'm not just losing the tax deduction, I'm losing what that tax deduction could have earned for me had I been able to invest that money elsewhere. That becomes a significant amount of money over time when you apply compounding interest to those losses. This is similar to pipes leaking under my house. If we discover there's a leaky pipe under our house and we just look at it and say, "Well that's not a big deal. I'm not going to mess with that," what would happen to our house? The damage would compound because we didn't repair the leaks in the pipes. There would be a huge devastation under the house. That's what's happening all across America today with dentists. They're realizing, "Wait a second, nobody told me my pipe was leaking and now the whole foundation of my retirement plan is rotten and devastated."

Nate: And this is why it's so hard for the dentists to get out of the chair?

Matt: Yes, it's simply because they do not have enough net worth that they can convert to cash flow to replace their current income. They simply don't have it. For instance, you asked about the million dollars in the 401(k). If a dentist brought a million dollars to me in a 401(k), what kind of income would that generate? Traditional financial planning would say that the dentist could take about 4% income and have a good chance of not running out of money. .

Four percent of a million dollars is forty thousand dollars. Dentists have a lifestyle of three, four or five hundred thousand dollars a year. They worked hard to try to save up a million dollars. Let's say they can sell their practice and get another million dollars. That's two million dollars. Before taxes on that income, you're looking at eighty thousand dollars a year of income. A dentist looks at that and says, "I don't want to live like that. I'm not going to live like that. I can't live like that. I can't live on eighty thousand dollars," and so they go in to the office every Monday with no real way to get out of the chair.

I met a dentist this year that is seventy-seven years old and still keeping a full schedule. He's saying, "I mean I love what I do as a dentist but the truth is I can't stop because I can't make this kind of money anywhere else. I don't have the net worth to support the kind of income I am used to."

Nate: Even if they had ten million I don't know if it would be enough.

Matt: Exactly. The Wharton School, one of the most prestigious business schools in America, just released a study this year and said for high-income earners, meaning those who make more than three hundred thousand dollars a year, to retire with the same amount of cash flow they have right now and not risk running out of money they need nineteen times their current income sitting in an account or sitting in a bucket if you will. Nineteen times three hundred thousand dollars is a lot of money. The dentists look at that and say, "There's no way I can get there."

Nate: They feel like the solution is to keep plugging away, keep working and hoping that someday they'll have enough in their buckets to meet the formula?

Matt: Here's the problem though. Many dental offices are only open three maybe four days a week. At first I thought that it was because those dentists just were making enough money and they wanted the freedom to take a day and a half a week and go play golf or do whatever they do, and some certainly do. For many of the dentists though, the reason that they're open three and a half, four days a week is because they're fifty, fifty-five, sixty years old and their bodies are breaking down from being hunched over working in patients mouths their whole career.

That day or day and half they are taking "off" is spent at the massage therapist or the chiropractor or just resting and recuperating because their body can't take the labor anymore. That's when they're getting really scared. They're fifty-five, sixty years old and saying, "Wait a second I don't know if my body can keep up. What am I going to do?" That's a real problem.

Nate: Well it surely is. What do the dentists need to know so that they can avoid this?

Matt: The first thing they need to know is that they have to look at their financial landscape in a totally different way. Like I said earlier, "They have to pay attention to the leaks." It really starts there, stopping the leaks. Most dentists are going to lose a million to two million dollars over their lifetime, just in the way that they finance their home. We need to stop that.

Most dentists are paying that much in taxes at the end of their life because they've got most of their money in their 401(k). So what we have to do is re-position those assets and go from making compartmentalized decisions to making coordinated financial decisions. My job as a financial adviser is never to tell any dentist what they need to do. My job is to ask them what they want to do and then to make sure that they understand what they are doing. I make it a habit to ask "What do you want to do? What are you doing and is what you are doing going to produce what you want? Is it really going to get you what you want?"

We really have to tell the truth and dive in and really look at what's happening. Really that's an education process. Nobody is going to care more about the dentist's money than the dentist themselves. I find it so interesting that dentists and most high-income earners are very in control of almost every area of their life. They have a philosophy. They have a thought process. They have energy towards every area of their life except this financial area. They say, "I don't really understand it. It's not what I do for a living. I'm just going to farm that out and I'll do annual meetings, but other than that I don't even want to think about it throughout the rest of the year."

A good education process, I believe, takes something that seems complex and makes it simple. I want dentists to learn that they don't need to know everything about financial planning; they just need to know a few things.

I am grateful to be a part of a group of advisors from around the country that have come together and started a wealth building movement; The Prosperity Economics Movement. Over the years, we have developed and implemented The 7 Principles of Prosperity.

These are simple principles I have vetted through my own experiences and the experiences of several hundred clients. If dentists will learn and apply these principles to their financial world, then they can begin to see a way out of the problem.

The real problem is we've got to get away from the bucket strategy and move to be more like the second businessman in our story; move to the pipeline strategy. To start, we need to look at what each dollar is doing and use the principles to get more out of each dollar.

The 7 Principles of Prosperity Every Dentist Should Know...

Prosperity Principle #1: THINK...Think Like an Entrepreneur

Nate: Let's talk about The 7 Principles dentists can use to get out of the chair.

Matt: The first principle that dentists need to embrace is to be what my friend Kim Butler calls an entrepreneurial thinker. Dentists and every business owner actually own two businesses. They own the one business that produces their cash and their income. That's the dental practice. Then they also own a second business that stores and invests that cash to create more future cash or more future cash flow. Every dentist must dedicate some time and energy to both of those businesses.

A dentist understands that if he's not in the chair Monday morning and he's not doing procedures that he's not going to be able to pay all of his staff and pay his bills and have a lifestyle at the end of the month. He understands that so he dedicates time and energy towards that. Well the same is true in his financial world. He needs to dedicate some time and energy getting educated to be an entrepreneurial thinker. An entrepreneurial thinker is focused not on trading time for money, but an entrepreneurial thinker is focused on results. The reason this is the number one principle is because there needs to be a mind shift, a shift into thinking about maximizing every transaction because we want to be results oriented.

When we're making coordinated financial decisions, that's really maximizing every transaction and being focused on results

Prosperity Principle #2: SEE...Avoid Financial Tunnel Vision...

The second principle is simply, do not be a victim of financial tunnel vision. Step back and see the big picture. Make coordinated financial decisions. See how every financial decision affects the other financial decisions in your life. If you are buried in a mortgage analysis, trying to decide on a 15 yr. or 30yr. mortgage, and that's all you are looking at, you make mistakes because you don't see how that decision impacts another area of you financial life. A wrong macroeconomic decision can have a million dollar impact on a person's financial world.

Prosperity Principle #3: MEASURE...Always Measure Opportunity Costs...

Number three is always, always, always measure opportunity costs. This principle is powerful because the miracle of compounding interest not only applies to our investments, it applies to our losses, as well. Opportunity costs are like a ball and chain on your money. For example, when you send a kid to college, you spend the money AND you lose the opportunity to use the money in your business or your retirement. You've lost that money for the rest of your life. In order to recover these costs, you have to first know where they are occurring. Measuring opportunity costs allows you to recover them. We've got to stop those losses.

Prosperity Principle #4: FLOW...Don't Focus on Net Worth alone...

Net worth is not the most valuable measure of wealth, cash flow is. Financial institutions want you to build that net worth so that they can turn it into cash flow, for them. What successful entrepreneurs, dentists and business owners need to do is build net worth in such a way that they can easily enhance their cash flow. Is there a way that we store cash in places that can help us focus on cash flow sooner rather than later?

Is the money in your 401(k)/profit sharing plan able to enhance your cash flow? Can you use it at all? Not without following some pretty stringent rules and not without paying taxes. This money in your 401(k) is simply idle net worth, not net worth that enhances cash flow. What's an example of net worth that enhances cash flow? If I had the 401(k) money, not in a 401(k), but in a place that I could borrow against using my cash as collateral, to open a second office which produces more income, then that worth, combined with a collateralized loan, enhanced my cash flow.

Prosperity Principle #5: CONTROL...Control of Your Capital Is More Important than Rate of Return...

The fifth principle is that control of your capital is more important than rate of return. The bucket strategy takes money out of your practice, out of your business, and puts it over here into this 401(k) or other before-tax qualified plan. Now you can't touch that money until at least age 59½ and probably don't want to touch until 65 or 70. The bucket strategy is to get it out of sight, out of mind. It'll earn a bunch of money over here and you'll be able to retire with that money. As you point out Nate, that is just not happening.

I believe that we need control and access to capital because there's no investment that I or any other adviser can bring to a dentist that offers him a higher rate of return than if he could just, in the safest possible way, reinvest back into his practice. That's where he's going to get his best rate of return. That's what he knows.

Why would I take money out of this practice, put it over into some kind of exotic investment that I don't know anything about but my broker told me, "Oh, it's going to get a good rate of return." Why would I do that versus reinvesting back into something that I know every in and out of. Control of your capital is very important. In fact, when I first meet a dentist or any business owner, I say to them, "Listen if I or any other adviser ever tells you I can make more money for you taking money out of your business and investing it somewhere else than you can make by reinvesting that money back in your business, then you need to run from me and run from that other adviser because that's just simply not true." We've got to have control of the capital.

Nate: Can you clarify something for me? Earlier you mentioned when the dentist goes to sell their practice they are only getting sixty to seventy cents on the dollar. So why are you saying they should invest back into a business they potentially are only going to be able to get sixty cents out of when they go to sell it later? What am I missing?

Matt: Thanks for clarifying that. What I mean by that is they should reinvest money into the business in such a way that it will increase cash flow back to them. The practice is only worth sixty to seventy cents on the dollar if I am viewing it as a bucket or accumulation vehicle that one day I'm going to sell to convert into retirement cash flow. The business right now is generating a much higher return on a month to month basis because it's generating a huge cash flow, enough to support a four or five hundred thousand dollar lifestyle.

If I had access to money, if I didn't have a million dollars in a 401(k) or other qualified plan and I had it somewhere else where I could access that money and use it to pay the first three months of three new associate doctor's salaries, it creates more cash flow in my business without me seeing any more patients personally. Now I can back down and eventually back out of the chair continuing to get the cash flow I was getting all along. The difference is now I don't have to be in the chair. I've got other people in the chair and I get to reap the benefit. That's creating the pipeline. When I view my practice as a pipeline, reinvesting money gets a huge return. When I view my practice as a bucket, reinvestment really creates a negative return.

Nate: By using their business as a pipeline they get immediate benefits not just twenty-five years from now? They get immediate cash flow now and you also have cash flow later when they want to step down or at least slow down?

Matt: That's exactly right. Thinking about their business as a pipeline very quickly allows the dentist to have freedom. And by freedom I mean choice, because a lot of dentists say, "You know I really love working on patients. I'd love to just do it one day a week." Okay, great they now have the freedom to do that. I've got other clients who say, "I can't stand it. I'm ready to get out of it. I don't want to ever touch a tooth again." Okay, great let's do that. You can have the freedom to choose how you want to spend your time.

I like to share with the dentists, "The pipeline strategy can allow you to retire in your business instead of having to retire from your business." It gives you the freedom. You're still the owner. You still reap the benefits of the cash flow, but you have the freedom to let other people generate that income instead of you having to be in the chair doing root canals, et cetera.

Prosperity Principle #6: MOVE...Act like a Bank...Move money through assets not to assets

For the next principle we need to understand what banks understand. Banks employ a financial principle called the velocity of money multiplier which simply means that money multiplies when it is in motion. What we need to do is move money through assets, not simply too assets.

To explain let's look at what a bank does and what a bank understands about your money. Their plan is really about control, they want us convinced they can give us our dream so they can gain financially by having control over our money. What does a bank do with your money when you deposit with them? Do they put it in a vault with your name on it and keep it there? No, they keep a very small amount in reserve, 10% or less depending on the reserve requirement for that bank and loan out the rest. They loan out your money on a credit card with 15% interest. When they get that money back, they loan it out on a boat at 9% interest. When they get that money back, they loan it out on a student loan at 4% interest. Most people understand that banks take your deposit and loan it out and earn the spread. What they do not understand is how they do this using the same dollar.

To illustrate this, let's say that a business owner obtains a loan of $10,000 at 8% to start a new venture. He uses the $10,000 to buy new office furniture and the furniture store takes the $10,000 he just gave them and deposits it in the same bank from which the original loan came from. If the bank has a reserve requirement of 10% then $9,000 of the furniture store's deposit now becomes loanable. So the bank loans $9,000 to an individual for a car at 6%. The car dealer deposits the $9,000 into the same bank of which the $8,100 is immediately loanable. This process continues through the year with $1 dollar being loaned several times with several different individuals paying interest to use it. The economic term for this is the multiplier effect. One dollar is moved through the system several times thereby multiplying the returns to the bank. Obviously, this strategy is very profitable for banks.

Are the financial institutions teaching you and me this strategy? No, they tell us to invest for the long term. They are not about helping us get truly wealthy, they are about controlling our money so they can multiply it for themselves. Here are the questions that you and I must ask ourselves. Are you going to be a customer of the bank? Or are you going to be the bank? Are you going follow the financial institution's advice? Or are you going to learn and apply the strategies they employ?

Prosperity Principle #7: MULTIPLY...Efficiency Allows Money to Multiply Many times Over...

Matt: The seventh principle is that efficiency allows money to multiply many times over. Money multiplies when one dollar does many jobs. Let me explain what I'm talking about there. The first thing we need to understand about this principle is that we want money to multiply, not just add. Let's think about these two equations, 3 x 3 and 3 + 3. Both use the same numbers but produce a different result. It's what you did with the numbers that produces the difference.

What are we doing with our money? What most people have is an inefficient financial world because they're compartmentalizing it. They've got dollars set aside for retirement. They've got dollars set aside for life insurance. They've got dollars for educating kids. They've got dollars that are paying a mortgage. They might be able to get a dollar to do two jobs.

For instance if I have a mortgage and I'm making that mortgage payment and the interest is tax deductible then those are doing two jobs. They're giving me a house and a place to live. I guess it's doing three jobs. It might be building equity in an asset, but then it provides a tax deduction so there are three jobs that those dollars are doing. When we use the bucket strategy and are compartmentalizing and are accumulating money in a bucket we're limiting the ability of the money to do more than one job. The question we need to ask is can I get one dollar, the same dollar to educate a child, to also get some insurance, to also possibly maybe buy investment real estate, to also reinvest back into the business and help me hire three or four associate dentists so that they can now take the pressure off me and I can multiply myself and my practice? Can I get the same dollar to do all those things?

Nate: Are you suggesting they don't use any buckets?

Matt: Remember, I believe that they need to build net worth but in such a way to enhance cash flow. So I'm suggesting that dentists use the Prosperity Principles to be selective. They use the principles to select places that they can store cash. First, they have to store cash and then they can deploy that cash into investments. The most fulfilling and successful investment is their business but we can have other cash flow producing investments as well. So we need to store cash in the most efficient way possible that gives us access to the money for use when opportunities arise. That's why I say, "We need to have assets but we need to have flow through assets not flow to assets."

Nate: Very good. Are dentists ever resistant to this do you find?

Matt: Yes, dentists are rule and protocol oriented. If you give them rules they want to follow those rules.

The problem has been they're following the wrong rules. The old rules aren't working and we've got to think about who taught them the rules? Dentists come out of school and they do what their dental school professors taught them about practicing and what their financial planners teach them about retirement planning. These planners teach them rules that are based on the rules that the financial institutions want them to know not what's really in their best interest. So the old rules don't work. Dentists are rule followers and what we're trying to do is to give them new rules to follow. These rules work. Those other rules don't work. These are the new rules. Dentists have been working with the wrong rules.

Nate: Very good. How risky is this Matt?

Matt: Following the 7 Principles of Prosperity reduces their risks, greatly. It lowers risk dramatically in two ways. First, when we store cash we want to use flow through assets that are guaranteed not to lose money and are protected from creditors. Second, when the time is right, we are moving money and re-investing it back into what they already know, their practice. I mean how risky is it to take money and give it to some money manager that lives in New York City or somewhere in the world that we don't even know, have never even seen before, can't even get on the phone and say, "Hey manage this portion of my money for me and give me a return." That's risk. That's crazy risk.

Even if they say, "Well we have a great track record." Well okay but how do I know that that's going to continue? So for the dentist, storing cash and then reinvesting it back into their business is something that they already know and understand. They understand how their business makes money. What we want to help them do is now just take that and multiply it and take it off of their back. Their business right now makes money on their back because they have to be in the chair earning money to pay everybody's salary and to support their lifestyle.

Nate: That is great because for some of the dentists, I would imagine, at first glance it may feel like, "I don't want to take on all these other people. It'll just be increasing my workload," but that's not what you're saying is it?

Matt: No, absolutely not. The new practice model you talk about can't be based on any one personality. What we're saying is transition your practice to a principal centered or a patient centered practice. I read a book called *Made to Stick*. In it the authors talk about when Southwest Airlines started, Herb Kelleher the CEO said, "Our mission, our number one guiding principle is we will be the low cost carrier in every market that we're in."

That became the filter now through which all other decisions were made. So when his marketing people came to him and said, "Hey listen we've done some surveys and our passengers want a chicken meal served to them on this flight because it's such a long distance." He looked at them and said, "Does serving that meal make us the low cost provider in that market?" They said, "No," and he said, "Great, well then we don't serve chicken meals." They came to him and said, "Hey listen we want to be fun and tell jokes on the airplanes and maybe even throw our flight attendants or our crew little birthdays parties on flights." He said, "Will that affect us being a low cost carrier in that market?" They said, "No." He said, "Great, well then do it," but he also said, "Don't throw confetti because then it's going to take time and effort and energy and ultimately money to clean it up."

The mission became the filter through which employees could make decisions. That's what we're trying to help dentists do, establish their own mission principle so that associates and staff can make decisions whether the doctor is there or not because they know the principle. Your mission principle is "What's best for the patient is best for the practice." That's like your Southwest Airlines mission statements. So if you're not there and the staff or the other associate doctors have to make a decision, they always know that, "What's best for the patient is best for the practice."

Nate: Can you share an example of a dentist you've worked with successfully?

Matt: Let's use you Nate. You've had twenty some odd years in dental practice doing exactly what all your financial planners said to do. You came to a place where you said, "This is not working. I don't want to continue to live like this." In fact you kind of entertained the thought of, "Gosh maybe I should just focus on other businesses and just shut this dental thing down because it's driving me crazy." But you looked at the cash flow and said, "Wait a second, it's producing too much cash flow. There's got to be a way to make this work."

That's when you started changing your mind set from Nate Schott the dentist to Nate Inc. and realized that the dental practice could become a self-managing business just like anything else. What we had to do was re-position cash flow and re-position assets. In the course of about a year of making the commitment to changing the way you were looking at financial planning and your practice you were totally out of the chair. You were able to totally step out and now you enjoy an incredible successful dental practice and you never have to touch a tooth.

You've replicated it at two other practices you've opened and you've got a third one coming on board. So you will have four practices by the middle of next year that you've replicated the model in. The size of your pipeline has grown dramatically.

Nate: Is this geographically limited Matt? Do they need to reside near you to take advantage of this?

Matt: No not at all. In fact we have dentists from Spokane, Washington, a dentist in San Francisco, a dentist in Phoenix, a dentist in New York City, a dentist on Long Island.

Nate: If they have further questions, how can they reach you?

Matt: They can call our office at: 615-295-8513 or email me at matt@next90coaching.com.

Nate: Thank you so much Matt for sharing this with us. I think the dentists are really going to get value from changing their business from bucket versus a pipeline.

Matt: My pleasure Nate. There is a better way to run their practice and I love helping them get there.

Here's How to Get Out of the Chair and Into Your Life...

You already know being a dentist can be brutal on the body. The confusing part is, not knowing the wealth building strategies that fly in the face of conventional wisdom.

That's where we come in. We help dentists just like you accelerate their wealth by using their practice to leverage the future they want and get out of the chair.

Step 1: We invest 60 minutes meeting with you to find your dangers, opportunities and strengths.

Step 2: We work with you and help you discover the key strategies the banks don't want you to know.

Step 3: We take it from here and take all your financial decisions and lay them out in a one page, easy to read format. This allows us to see at a glance where the gaps are in your financial plan.

Most dentists think it takes serious capital for wealth-building, built up over years and years of being in the chair.

Now you can make your greatest asset work for you now not 25 years down the road and get out of the chair once and for all.

If you'd like us to help, just send an email to: matt@next90coaching.com and we will take it from there.

About the Authors

Matt Kennedy has been assisting people with their financial services needs since 1997. Upon graduation from Union University, Matt began helping clients protect their personal and business assets. His easy-going personality and knack for clearly explaining complicated issues, helped make him a trusted advisor to a large number of clients around the U.S..

After a 5 year period on staff with the Young Life ministry, Matt returned to the financial arena with a new focus: teaching clients how to eliminate financial decisions that could be transferring away their wealth. Through extensive education, Matt teaches clients a holistic approach to financial management. He teaches clients how every financial decision is an important one that has a ripple effect throughout their entire life

Matt says, "Do you remember the first time you played Tic Tac Toe? I'll bet you lost. I'll even bet that you lost regularly until someone taught you the rules of the game. The financial world is no different. There are rules that no one is teaching you. My job is not to play the financial game for you but to teach you the rules of the game so that you can play more efficiently and create a more financially independent future."

Most recently, Matt has partnered with a Dr. Nate Schott to create Partners in Dental Excellence. Through Partners in Dental Excellence, Matt and Nate works with dentists around the country with a passionate mission; "Get out of the chair and get into your life!"

Nate Schott, DDS is a dentist on a mission to help as many people as possible improve their oral health by becoming better informed dental consumers. Dr. Nate attended Carson-Newman University where he majored in Biology, and he is a 1991 graduate of the University of Tennessee College of Dentistry. He is an industry leader in continuing education, policy, and procedural issues. He has lectured extensively throughout the United States and abroad, dedicating his professional career to providing the best dentistry has to offer.

In addition to owning Murfreesboro Dental Excellence, a growing dental practice in Murfreesboro, Tennessee, Dr. Nate is an entrepreneur by nature. He is the creator and owner of *Dr. Nate's Naturals*, an all-natural oral health care product line. He is also a co-founding investor in the Trustpoint Hospital Corporation, which provides in-patient rehabilitation and behavioral services through its facilities in Murfreesboro and Lubbock, Texas. Dr. Nate also consults and trains dentists by providing valuable tools to doctor/ owners who are seeking to expand and increase practice access, affordability and growth.

www.ingramcontent.com/pod-product-compliance
Lightning Source LLC
Chambersburg PA
CBHW070722180526
45167CB00004B/1577